I0782133

BECOMING INTENTIONAL

12-Month Empowerment Journal

JOANNE M. CHERISMA

A MONTHLY GUIDE TO…
BECOMING INTENTIONAL

HOV Publishing is a division of HOV, LLC.
Bridgeport, CT 06605
Email: hopeofvision@gmail.com
www.90daybookcreation.com

Cover Design and Layout: Canva and HOV Designs
Editors: HOV Publishing editing team

Contact the Author:
Joanne M. Cherisma
info@joannemcherisma.com

For further information regarding special discounts on bulk purchases, please contact: Joanne M. Cherisma at info@joannemcherisma.com.

ISBN Hard Case: 978-1-955107-42-6

Printed in the United States of America

DEDICATION

To You,

As you take steps toward Becoming Intentional,

developing a positive and clear mindset, reaching

your goals and purpose, and being more present, may

your body be transformed and your mind empowered.

TABLE OF CONTENTS

HOW TO USE THIS GUIDE

1. **Summary**

   Author Joanne M. Cherisma shares her personal experiences each month in "Becoming Intentional," aiming to empower readers with insightful themes and lessons.

   Each month begins with an introduction to its specific theme, providing context and a preview of the journey ahead. This section helps set the tone and focus for the month's explorations and activities.

2. **Call to Action**

   Engage in activities and reflections that encourage the practice of each monthly theme in personal, professional, and spiritual areas. These actionable steps are designed to integrate the theme into various aspects of your life.

3. **General Questions for Weekly Actions**

   Reflective questions are provided to prompt deeper thought and application of the monthly theme in your weekly activities. These questions are intended to guide and enhance your weekly focus.

4. **Weekly Focus**

   Each week of the month is given a specific focus, aligning with the overall theme. This breakdown helps in maintaining a consistent engagement with the theme throughout the month.
   - Week 1:
   - Week 2:

- Week 3:
- Week 4:
- Week 5: (For months with five weeks)

5. Personal Goals

Track three personal goals related to the theme of the month. Reflect on how these goals were inspired by the monthly theme and weekly actions. This section is crucial for setting intentions and measuring progress.

6. Blank Monthly Calendar

A blank calendar is provided for each month to help you plan and track your activities, reflections, and progress. Use this space to schedule time for the Call-to-Action activities, note important dates, and jot down insights and achievements related to the monthly theme.

7. Notes

This section is dedicated to your personal thoughts, observations, and reflections. It's a space for you to write down insights, break-throughs, challenges faced, and lessons learned throughout the month. It can be used for journaling, doodling, brainstorming, or any other form of personal expression that supports your journey with the monthly theme.

BOLDNESS

Boldness is often one of the first qualities to emerge during personal transformation. Initially, individuals may find themselves shrouded in fear, seeking solace in contemplation and mutual support. However, through a transformative process, a shift occurs, instilling a sense of fearlessness. This kind of boldness is more than a mere personality trait; it signifies the courage to stand firm in one's convictions, even in the face of challenges or threats. Such boldness can be distilled into three key elements: a deeply held conviction, reinforced by courage and a sense of urgency.

Let's embark on a journey to experience and embody boldness in our daily lives.

- ***Understanding Boldness:*** *Explore the perspective of boldness as an act of faith and not merely a personality trait. Reflect on how this can be applied in modern contexts.*

____

____

____

____

____

____

____

CALL TO ACTION

Engage in activities and reflections that encourage the practice of
boldness in these three areas of your life:

Personal: ____

____

____

____

Professional: ____

____

____

____

Spiritual: ____

____

____

____

GENERAL QUESTIONS FOR WEEKLY ACTION

How did I practice spiritual boldness this week in a situation that challenged my faith or convictions?

DAYS	WHAT WAS CHALLENGED?	DID I PRACTICE BOLDNESS?
SUNDAY		
MONDAY		
TUESDAY		
WEDNESDAY		
THURSDAY		
FRIDAY		
SATURDAY		

WEEK 1: Identifying Areas for Boldness.

Personal: ____

____

____

____

Professional: ____

____

____

____

Spiritual: ____

____

____

____

WEEK 2: Developing Conviction and Courage.

Personal: ____

____

____

____

____

Professional: ____

____

____

____

____

Spiritual: ____

____

____

____

WEEK 3: Overcoming Fear with Faith.

Personal: ____

____

____

____

____

Professional: ____

____

____

____

____

Spiritual: ____

____

____

____

WEEK 4: Implementing Bold Actions.

Personal: ____

____

____

____

____

Professional: ____

____

____

____

____

Spiritual: ____

____

____

____

WEEK 5: Reflecting and Building Upon Boldness Achieved. (For 5-week months)

Personal: ____

____

____

____

Professional: ____

____

____

____

Spiritual: ____

____

____

____

Track three personal goals related to the theme of boldness for the month. Encourage reflection on how these goals were inspired by the monthly theme and weekly actions.

Goal 1: ____

____

____

____

Goal 2: ____

____

____

____

Goal 3: ____

____

____

____

CALENDAR

MONTH/YEAR: _______________

Sunday	Monday	Tuesday	Wednesday	Thursday	Friday	Saturday

- NOTES -

FORGIVENESS

Forgiveness is an intentional and voluntary process in which an individual experiences a change in feelings and attitude concerning an offense. It involves a conscious decision to release negative thoughts, such as revenge, and cultivate the capacity to wish well for the offender. Importantly, forgiveness is distinct from condoning, excusing, forgetting, pardoning, or reconciling. At various points in our lives, we find ourselves in need of forgiveness. Reflecting on my own experiences, I recognize the numerous times I've faltered and required forgiveness. It prompts a critical question: how can I expect forgiveness from others if I'm not practicing it myself? Therefore, extending forgiveness is essential for receiving it, particularly if I seek to embrace all that God has in store for me. While I can't erase past memories, I've learned that I do have control over my present actions. Hence, my approach to forgiveness is intentional, not merely optional. I choose love over bitterness, recognizing that to move forward, I must let go and free myself.

JOIN THE JOURNEY

Embark on a journey of releasing bitterness and choosing love, learning to let go and free ourselves for a fuller, more intentional life.

- ***Exploring Forgiveness:*** *Reflect on the nature of forgiveness, its importance in our lives, and how it differs from other responses to offense.*

____

____

____

____

____

____

____

____

CALL TO ACTION

Engage in activities and reflections that encourage practicing forgiveness in personal, professional, and spiritual realms.

Personal: ____

____

____

____

Professional: ____

____

____

____

Spiritual: ____

____

____

____

GENERAL QUESTIONS FOR WEEKLY ACTION

How did I practice forgiveness this week in a situation that previously caused me hurt or anger?

DAYS	WHAT CAUSED PAIN OR HURT?	DID I PRACTICE FORGIVENESS?
SUNDAY		
MONDAY		
TUESDAY		
WEDNESDAY		
THURSDAY		
FRIDAY		
SATURDAY		

WEEK 1: Recognizing the Need for Forgiveness.

Personal: ____

____

____

____

Professional: ____

____

____

____

Spiritual: ____

____

____

____

WEEK 2: Understanding the Impact of Holding onto Hurt.

Personal: ____

____

____

____

____

Professional: ____

____

____

____

____

Spiritual: ____

____

____

____

WEEK 3: Steps Towards Forgiving Others.

Personal: ____

____

____

____

Professional: ____

____

____

____

____

Spiritual: ____

____

____

____

WEEK 4: Embracing Forgiveness as a Path to Freedom.

Personal: ____

____

____

____

____

Professional: ____

____

____

____

____

Spiritual: ____

____

____

____

WEEK 5: Reflecting on the Journey of Forgiveness.

(For 5-week months)

Personal: ____

____

____

____

____

Professional: ____

____

____

____

Spiritual: ____

____

____

____

Track three personal goals related to the theme of forgiveness for the month. Encourage reflection on how these goals were inspired by the monthly theme and weekly actions.

Goal 1: ____

____

____

____

Goal 2: ____

____

____

____

Goal 3: ____

____

____

____

CALENDAR

MONTH/YEAR: _______________

Sunday	Monday	Tuesday	Wednesday	Thursday	Friday	Saturday

- NOTES -

- MARCH -
SELF-LOVE

To love others and the world around you, the journey begins with loving YOURSELF. You can't give what you don't have; only what you possess within. Remember, you are wonderful, and crafted beautifully, and always be grateful for your blessings. Embrace life with enthusiasm. Take a moment to slow down, enjoy the now while thoughtfully considering the future. Strive to be kind, smart, creative, fantastic, unstoppable, strong, and resilient. And always, remember to:

- Love YOURSELF.

- Take care of YOURSELF.

- Celebrate YOURSELF.

- Forgive YOURSELF.

- Be at peace with YOURSELF.

Let's embrace the journey of **self-love**, learning to love, care for, celebrate, forgive, and be at peace with ourselves.

- ***Embracing Self-Love:*** *Explore the importance of self-love and how it influences our interactions with others and our overall well-being.*

____

____

____

____

____

____

____

____

CALL TO ACTION

Engage in activities and reflections that foster self-love, self-acceptance, and self-care in our daily lives.

Personal: ____

____

____

____

Professional: ____

____

____

____

Spiritual: ____

____

____

____

GENERAL QUESTIONS FOR WEEKLY ACTION

What actions did I take this week to demonstrate love and care for yourself?

DAYS	WHAT WAS THE ACTION?	HOW DID I DEMONSTRATE LOVE AND CARE?
SUNDAY		
MONDAY		
TUESDAY		
WEDNESDAY		
THURSDAY		
FRIDAY		
SATURDAY		

WEEKLY FOCUS

WEEK 1: Understanding Self-Love.

Personal: ____

____

____

____

Professional: ____

____

____

____

Spiritual: ____

____

____

____

WEEK 2: Practicing Gratitude and Appreciation for Oneself.

Personal: ____

____

____

____

____

Professional: ____

____

____

____

____

Spiritual: ____

____

____

____

WEEK 3: Self-Care and Celebrating Personal Achievements.

Personal: _______________________________________

____

____

____

____

Professional: _______________________________________

____

____

____

____

Spiritual: _______________________________________

____

____

____

WEEK 4: Forgiving and Being at Peace with Oneself.

Personal: ____

____

____

____

____

Professional: ____

____

____

____

____

Spiritual: ____

____

____

____

WEEK 5: Reflecting on the Growth in Self-Love
Achieved. (For 5-week months)

Personal: _______________________________________

____

____

____

Professional: ___________________________________

____

____

____

____

Spiritual: _______________________________________

____

____

____

PERSONAL GOALS

Track three personal goals related to the theme of self-love for the month. Encourage reflection on how these goals align with and enhance your journey of self-love.

Goal 1: ____

____

____

____

Goal 2: ____

____

____

____

Goal 3: ____

____

____

____

CALENDAR

MONTH/YEAR: ______________

Sunday	Monday	Tuesday	Wednesday	Thursday	Friday	Saturday

- NOTES -

- APRIL -

PERSEVERANCE

On our journey of recovery, we will encounter many obstacles, some greater than others. Yet, as we overcome each one, we find ourselves rising, standing taller with each victory. At the journey's end, there shines a light, reachable only through perseverance, despite the many challenges - the setbacks, the failures, the oppositions, the delays, the loneliness, and the rejections. True prosperity is the reward of those who steadfastly refuse to give up. Stay steady, continue even when faced with discouragement, and embrace strength in sometimes walking the path alone.

This month, let's commit to staying steady, persisting despite discouragement, and embracing the courage to sometimes walk alone.

- ***The Essence of Perseverance:*** *Explore the importance of perseverance in overcoming life's challenges and the qualities that define a persevering spirit.*

____

____

____

____

____

____

____

____

Engage in activities and reflections that cultivate resilience, determination, and the ability to face adversities with a positive mindset.

Personal: ____

____

____

____

Professional: ____

____

____

____

Spiritual: ____

____

____

____

GENERAL QUESTIONS FOR WEEKLY ACTION

What challenges did I face this week and how did I demonstrate perseverance in dealing with them.

DAYS	WHAT CHALLENGES DID I FACE?	DID I PRACTICE PERSEVERANCE?
SUNDAY		
MONDAY		
TUESDAY		
WEDNESDAY		
THURSDAY		
FRIDAY		
SATURDAY		

WEEK 1: Identifying Personal Obstacles.

Personal: _______________________________________

____

____

____

Professional: _______________________________________

____

____

____

Spiritual: _______________________________________

____

____

____

WEEK 2: Building Resilience against Failures.

Personal: ____

____

____

____

____

Professional: ____

____

____

____

____

Spiritual: ____

____

____

____

WEEK 3: Maintaining Momentum in the Face of Opposition.

Personal: _______________________________________

____

____

____

Professional: _______________________________________

____

____

____

Spiritual: _______________________________________

____

____

____

WEEK 4: Finding Strength in Solitude and Delay.

Personal: ____

____

____

____

Professional: ____

____

____

____

Spiritual: ____

____

____

____

WEEK 5: Reflecting on the Triumphs of Perseverance.
(For 5-week months)

Personal: ____

____

____

____

____

Professional: _______________________________________

____

____

____

____

Spiritual: ____

____

____

____

PERSONAL GOALS

Track three personal goals related to the theme of perseverance for the month. Encourage reflection on how these goals embody the spirit of perseverance and contribute to personal growth.

Goal 1: ____

____

____

____

Goal 2: ____

____

____

____

Goal 3: ____

____

____

____

CALENDAR

MONTH/YEAR: _______________

Sunday	Monday	Tuesday	Wednesday	Thursday	Friday	Saturday

- NOTES -

TRUST

I came to realize and accept the fact that I wasn't in control of my life. No matter the extent of my planning, and the hours of effort I put in, all I could do was my very best and entrust the rest to God. My reliance on Him stemmed from His proven, unconditional love, reassuring me that He desires only the best for me. Therefore, I have no choice but to trust Him. This trust extends to believing in the abilities He has given me to achieve what seems impossible. So, whenever I'm asked how I do it all, my simple response is: "It's not just me; it's God working through me."

Embrace a month of learning to **trust** beyond our understanding and capabilities, acknowledging that sometimes, "God is doing it."

- ***Exploring the Depth of Trust:*** *Reflect on the nature of trust in a higher power and in our own abilities, and how this trust can transform our approach to life and challenges.*

____

____

____

____

____

____

____

____

CALL TO ACTION

Engage in activities and reflections that foster a deeper sense of **trust**, surrender, and reliance on a power greater than ourselves.

Personal: ____

____

____

____

Professional: ____

____

____

Spiritual: ____

____

____

____

GENERAL QUESTIONS FOR WEEKLY ACTION

How did I demonstrate trust in God and in myself in the face of uncertainty this week?

DAYS	WHAT WAS CHALLENGED?	HOW DID YOU DEMONSTRATE TRUST IN GOD?
SUNDAY		
MONDAY		
TUESDAY		
WEDNESDAY		
THURSDAY		
FRIDAY		
SATURDAY		

WEEK 1: Understanding the Role of Trust in Life.

Personal: ____

____

____

____

Professional: ____

____

____

____

Spiritual: ____

____

____

____

WEEK 2: Learning to Let Go and Trust the Process.

Personal: ____

____

____

____

____

Professional: ____

____

____

____

Spiritual: ____

____

____

____

WEEK 3: Building Trust in Personal Abilities and Divine Guidance.

Personal: _______________________________________

____

____

____

____

Professional: _______________________________________

____

____

____

Spiritual: _______________________________________

____

____

____

WEEK 4: Experiencing the Peace that Comes with Trust.

Personal: ____

____

____

____

____

Professional: ____

____

____

____

Spiritual: ____

____

____

____

WEEK 5: Reflecting on the Growth and Insights Gained through Trust. (For 5-week months)

Personal: ____

____

____

____

____

Professional: ____

____

____

____

Spiritual: ____

____

____

____

PERSONAL GOALS

Track three personal goals related to the theme of **trust** for the month.
Encourage reflection on how these goals are influenced by the
newfound understanding and practice of trust.

Goal 1: ____

____

____

____

Goal 2: ____

____

____

____

Goal 3: ____

____

____

____

CALENDAR

MONTH/YEAR: ______________

Sunday	Monday	Tuesday	Wednesday	Thursday	Friday	Saturday

- NOTES -

GRATEFULNESS

Embarking on this journey has given me the opportunity of meeting so many strong people, exploring different places, and hearing so many incredible stories. These experiences have allowed me to realize how blessed I am. Each morning, as I wake up, I express thanks to God for the gift of life, often overlooking the simple yet profound fact that I am breathing, walking independently, using my hands, and sharing smiles with my bright teeth. These stories have increased my appreciation for my own life like never before. Each day, I'm learning to be more thankful for what I already have while I continue to chase my dreams. Even if God grants me nothing more, may I forever remain grateful for what I already have.

Let's embrace a month of gratitude, learning to be increasingly thankful for the present blessings, regardless of what the future holds.

- ***Celebrating Gratefulness:*** *Explore the power of gratitude in transforming our perspective on life and enhancing our overall well-being.*

____

____

____

____

____

____

____

____

____

CALL TO ACTION

Engage in activities and reflections that cultivate a sense of gratefulness for the many blessings, both big and small, in our lives.

Personal: ____

____

____

____

Professional: ____

____

____

____

Spiritual: ____

____

____

____

What moments or aspects of my life did I feel grateful for this week?

DAYS	WHAT MOMENTS WERE I CHALLENGED?	DID I FEEL GRATEFUL?
SUNDAY		
MONDAY		
TUESDAY		
WEDNESDAY		
THURSDAY		
FRIDAY		
SATURDAY		

WEEK 1: Acknowledging Daily Blessings.

Personal: ____

____

____

____

Professional: ____

____

____

____

Spiritual: ____

____

____

____

WEEK 2: Learning from Others' Stories of Strength
and Gratitude.

Personal: _______________________________________

____

____

____

Professional: ___________________________________

____

____

____

Spiritual: ______________________________________

____

____

____

WEEK 3: Appreciating the Simple Joys of Life.

Personal: _______________________________________

____

____

____

____

Professional: _______________________________________

____

____

____

____

Spiritual: _______________________________________

____

____

____

WEEK 4: Integrating Gratefulness into Daily Practices.

Personal: ____

____

____

____

Professional: _______________________________________

____

____

____

____

Spiritual: ____

____

____

____

WEEK 5: Reflecting on the Transformative Power of Gratitude. (For 5-week months)

Personal: _______________________________________

____

____

____

Professional: _______________________________________

____

____

____

Spiritual: _______________________________________

____

____

____

PERSONAL GOALS

Track three personal goals related to the theme of gratefulness for the month. Encourage reflection on how these goals are influenced by and contribute to a deeper sense of gratitude.

Goal 1: ____

____

____

____

Goal 2: ____

____

____

____

Goal 3: ____

____

____

____

CALENDAR

MONTH/YEAR: _______________

Sunday	Monday	Tuesday	Wednesday	Thursday	Friday	Saturday

- NOTES -

CONSISTENCY

The dictionary describes consistency as "the achievement of a level of performance that does not vary greatly over time." This principle holds immense power. Indeed, the essence of success lies in consistency. It demands diligent effort and plays a crucial role in building trust. Ultimately, it's this consistent hard work that paves the way to success.

Let's dedicate this month to developing and reinforcing consistent practices in all areas of our lives.

- ***The Power of Consistency:*** *Explore the importance of consistency in achieving long-term success and how it can be applied in various aspects of life.*

____

____

____

____

____

____

____

CALL TO ACTION

Engage in activities and reflections that help establish and maintain consistent behaviors and routines.

Personal: _______________________________________

____

____

____

Professional: _______________________________________

____

____

____

Spiritual: _______________________________________

____

____

____

GENERAL QUESTIONS FOR WEEKLY ACTION

What consistent actions did I take this week towards achieving my goals?

DAYS	WHAT WERE THE CONSISTENT ACTIONS?	DID I ACHIEVE MY GOAL?
SUNDAY		
MONDAY		
TUESDAY		
WEDNESDAY		
THURSDAY		
FRIDAY		
SATURDAY		

WEEK 1: Understanding the Role of Consistency in Success.

Personal: ____

____

____

____

Professional: ____

____

____

____

Spiritual: ____

____

____

____

WEEK 2: Building and Maintaining Consistent Habits.

Personal: ____

____

____

____

Professional: ____

____

____

____

Spiritual: ____

____

____

____

WEEK 3: Overcoming Challenges to Consistency.

Personal: ____

____

____

____

____

Professional: ____

____

____

____

Spiritual: ____

____

____

____

WEEK 4: Measuring and Celebrating Consistent Efforts.

Personal: ____

____

____

____

____

Professional: ____

____

____

____

Spiritual: ____

____

____

____

WEEK 5: Reflecting on the Impact of Consistency on Personal Growth. (For 5-week months)

Personal: ____

____

____

____

____

Professional: ____

____

____

____

____

Spiritual: ____

____

____

____

PERSONAL GOALS

Track three personal goals related to the theme of consistency for the month. Encourage reflection on how these goals align with the principle of consistency.

Goal 1: ____

____

____

____

Goal 2: ____

____

____

____

Goal 3: ____

____

____

____

CALENDAR

MONTH/YEAR: _______________

Sunday	Monday	Tuesday	Wednesday	Thursday	Friday	Saturday

- NOTES -

- AUGUST -

PATIENCE

Waiting, staying calm, and enduring the process can be challenging, but the outcome is often worth the wait. Patience is a strength, urging us not to hurry. Remember, good things need time to unfold. During the wait, let's stay focused and maintain a positive attitude.

Let's spend this month cultivating patience, understanding that good things often take time and that our attitude during the wait is as important as the outcome.

- ***Exploring the Essence of Patience:*** *Reflect on the importance of patience in personal growth and achievement, and how it can positively impact various areas of life.*

____

____

____

____

____

____

____

CALL TO ACTION

Engage in activities and reflections that encourage the development and practice of patience in daily life:

Personal: ____

____

____

____

Professional: ____

____

____

____

Spiritual: ____

____

____

____

How did I practice patience this week in situations that tested my ability to wait and remain calm?

DAYS	WHAT SITUATIONS TESTED ME?	DID I PRACTICE PATIENCE?
SUNDAY		
MONDAY		
TUESDAY		
WEDNESDAY		
THURSDAY		
FRIDAY		
SATURDAY		

WEEK 1: Recognizing the Value of Patience.

Personal: ____

____

____

____

Professional: ____

____

____

____

Spiritual: ____

____

____

____

WEEK 2: Learning to Embrace the Process.

Personal: _______________________________________

____

____

____

____

Professional: _______________________________________

____

____

____

____

Spiritual: _______________________________________

____

____

____

WEEK 3: Cultivating a Positive Attitude in Waiting.

Personal: ________________________

____

____

____

____

Professional: ________________________

____

____

____

____

Spiritual: ________________________

____

____

____

WEEK 4: Overcoming Impatience and Frustration.

Personal: _______________________________________

____

____

____

____

Professional: _______________________________________

____

____

____

____

Spiritual: _______________________________________

____

____

____

WEEK 5: Reflecting on the Growth Gained Through Patience. (For 5-week months)

Personal: ____

____

____

____

____

Professional: ____

____

____

____

Spiritual: ____

____

____

____

PERSONAL GOALS

Track three personal goals related to the theme of patience for the month. Encourage reflection on how practicing patience contributes to achieving these goals and overall well-being.

Goal 1: ____

____

____

____

Goal 2: ____

____

____

____

Goal 3: ____

____

____

____

CALENDAR

MONTH/YEAR: ______________

Sunday	Monday	Tuesday	Wednesday	Thursday	Friday	Saturday

- NOTES -

SELF-REFLECTION

Discovering an old photograph recently, it brought back so many memories. In this moment it made me realize the vital role of self-reflection in personal growth. Sometimes, it's necessary to pause and re-evaluate our direction to stay on track. As John Dewey said: "We do not learn from experience; we learn from reflecting on experience." This self-awareness allows us to evolve into healthier individuals. To truly transform, we must first make peace with our reflections in the mirror.

Embrace a month dedicated to introspection, personal growth, and the transformative power of self-reflection.

- ***The Importance of Self-Reflection:*** *Explore the concept of self-reflection, its benefits, and how it contributes to personal development and emotional well-being.*

____

____

____

____

____

____

____

____

CALL TO ACTION

Engage in activities and reflections that promote deeper self-awareness and understanding:

Personal: ____

____

____

____

Professional: ____

____

____

____

Spiritual: ____

____

____

____

What did I learn about myself this week through self-reflection?

DAYS	WHAT DID I LEARN?	DID I USE SELF-REFLECTION?
SUNDAY		
MONDAY		
TUESDAY		
WEDNESDAY		
THURSDAY		
FRIDAY		
SATURDAY		

WEEK 1: Understanding the Role of Self-Reflection
in Growth.

Personal: _______________________________________

____

____

____

Professional: _______________________________________

____

____

____

Spiritual: _______________________________________

____

____

____

WEEK 2: Reflecting on Past Experiences and Their Lessons.

Personal: ____

____

____

____

Professional: ____

____

____

____

Spiritual: ____

____

____

____

WEEK 3: Assessing Current Thoughts, Feelings, and Behaviors.

Personal: ____

____

____

____

____

Professional: ____

____

____

____

____

Spiritual: ____

____

____

____

WEEK 4: Setting Intentions for Future Based on Reflections.

Personal: ____

____

____

____

____

Professional: ____

____

____

____

Spiritual: ____

____

____

____

WEEK 5: Integrating Reflections into Personal and Spiritual
Life. (For 5-week months)

Personal: ____

____

____

____

____

Professional: ____

____

____

____

____

Spiritual: ____

____

____

____

PERSONAL GOALS

Track three personal goals related to the theme of self-reflection for the month. Encourage reflection on how these goals are shaped by insights gained through self-reflection.

Goal 1: ____

____

____

____

Goal 2: ____

____

____

____

Goal 3: ____

____

____

____

CALENDAR

MONTH/YEAR: _______________

Sunday	Monday	Tuesday	Wednesday	Thursday	Friday	Saturday

- NOTES -

MATURATION

To grow and evolve, embracing change is essential. This process requires patience, a willingness to learn from our mistakes, and a commitment to developing wisdom. It's also about letting go of the past and embracing our future. This doesn't mean we forget where we came from; rather, it means that we're not held captive by our past. We are free to move forward.

Embrace a month of growth, change, and the beauty of becoming, as we each evolve into our best selves.

- ***Understanding Maturation:*** *Explore the process of maturation, its importance in personal development, and the balance between honoring the past and embracing the future.*

____

____

____

____

____

____

____

____

CALL TO ACTION

Engage in activities and reflections that support growth, change, and the shedding of past limitations:

Personal: ____

____

____

____

Professional: ____

____

____

____

Spiritual: ____

____

____

____

What steps did I take this week towards personal growth and maturation?

DAYS	DID I TAKE STEPS TOWARDS PERSONAL GROWTH?	WHAT AREAS DID I GROW IN?
SUNDAY		
MONDAY		
TUESDAY		
WEDNESDAY		
THURSDAY		
FRIDAY		
SATURDAY		

WEEK 1: Embracing Change for Growth.

Personal: ____

____

____

____

Professional: ____

____

____

____

Spiritual: ____

____

____

____

WEEK 2: Learning from Mistakes and Building Wisdom.

Personal: ____

____

____

____

____

Professional: ____

____

____

____

____

Spiritual: ____

____

____

____

WEEK 3: Letting Go of the Past.

Personal: ____

____

____

____

____

Professional: ____

____

____

____

Spiritual: ____

____

____

____

WEEK 4: Welcoming the Future with Openness and Hope.

Personal: ___________________________

____

____

____

____

Professional: ___________________________

____

____

____

____

Spiritual: ___________________________

____

____

____

WEEK 5: Celebrating the New Self Emerging.
(For 5-week months)

Personal: ____

____

____

____

____

Professional: ____

____

____

____

Spiritual: ____

____

____

____

Track three personal goals related to the theme of maturation for the month. Encourage reflection on how these goals reflect the process of evolving and maturing.

Goal 1: ____

____

____

____

Goal 2: ____

____

____

____

Goal 3: ____

____

____

____

CALENDAR

MONTH/YEAR: _______________

Sunday	Monday	Tuesday	Wednesday	Thursday	Friday	Saturday

- NOTES -

- NOVEMBER -

RECOVERY

There are moments when slowing down, taking a break, or even stopping to reconsider your journey is necessary. Life is about achieving balance. Sometimes, it is only when you take a moment to pause and evaluate your own needs that you come to understand you've been overwhelmed. In the pursuit of recovery, remember that rest and self-care are just as important as everything else. Dedicate time to renewing your spirit and remember that you can't give what you don't have.

Let's dedicate this month to the process of recovery, focusing on rest, self-care, and rejuvenation.

- ***Embracing the Process of Recovery:*** *Reflect on the importance of recovery in our lives, the role of rest and self-care, and the balance they bring.*

____

____

____

____

____

____

____

____

CALL TO ACTION

Engage in activities and reflections that focus on self-recovery, rest, and replenishment of the spirit:

Personal: ____

____

____

____

Professional: ____

____

____

____

Spiritual: ____

____

____

____

GENERAL QUESTIONS FOR WEEKLY ACTION

What actions did I take this week to aid my personal recovery and well-being?

DAYS	WHAT ACTION DID I TAKE?	HOW DID IT AID IN MY PERSONAL RECOVERY?
SUNDAY		
MONDAY		
TUESDAY		
WEDNESDAY		
THURSDAY		
FRIDAY		
SATURDAY		

WEEK 1: Recognizing the Need for Recovery.

Personal: ____

____

____

____

Professional: ____

____

____

____

Spiritual: ____

____

____

____

WEEK 2: Implementing Rest and Self-Care Practices.

Personal: ____

____

____

____

____

Professional: ____

____

____

____

____

Spiritual: ____

____

____

____

WEEK 3: Listening to and Understanding Personal Needs.

Personal: ____

____

____

____

____

Professional: ____

____

____

____

____

Spiritual: ____

____

____

____

WEEK 4: Reflecting on the Benefits of Recovery.

Personal: ____

____

____

____

____

Professional: _______________________________________

____

____

____

____

Spiritual: ____

____

____

____

WEEK 5: Planning for Continued Wellness and Recovery.
(For 5-week months)

Personal: ____

____

____

____

Professional: ____

____

____

____

Spiritual: ____

____

____

____

PERSONAL GOALS

Track three personal goals related to the theme of recovery for the month. Encourage reflection on how these goals align with the journey of personal recovery and balance.

Goal 1: ____

____

____

____

Goal 2: ____

____

____

____

Goal 3: ____

____

____

____

CALENDAR

MONTH/YEAR: _______________

Sunday	Monday	Tuesday	Wednesday	Thursday	Friday	Saturday

- NOTES -

- DECEMBER -
FULFILLMENT

Sometimes, we only hear and see what we want until reality hits us. Throughout the year, in the whirlwind of days, events, and opportunities, I overlooked crucial signs urging me to slow down. It took a real challenging recovery and a series of uncomfortable situations to help me understand that my inability to call things as they are, wasn't a sign of weakness. It was simply part of being human.

To turn the page on this chapter of my life, I had to accept that my tears were not a sign of weakness, but a natural response to pain. Yet, my resilience to rise and dust myself off triumphs over everything. This year has been a journey of living, loving, losing, missing, hurting, trusting, making mistakes, and above all, I have learned. I am now ready to move forward again, welcoming the upcoming year, new beginnings, being human, embracing smiles, gaining knowledge, and growing wiser.

Celebrate a month of fulfillment, reflecting on the past year's journey and looking forward to new beginnings with wisdom and a renewed spirit.

- ***Reflecting on a Year of Growth:*** *Explore the various experiences of the past year and how they contribute to a sense of fulfillment and readiness for the future.*

____

____

____

____

____

____

____

____

CALL TO ACTION

Engage in activities and reflections that celebrate the year's achievements, lessons, and personal growth:

Personal: ____

____

____

____

Professional: ____

____

____

____

Spiritual: ____

____

____

____

GENERAL QUESTIONS FOR WEEKLY ACTION

How did my experiences this week contribute to my sense of fulfillment and readiness for the new year?

DAYS	WHAT WAS MY EXPERIENCE THIS WEEK?	DID IT CONTRIBUTE TO MY FULFILLMENT?
SUNDAY		
MONDAY		
TUESDAY		
WEDNESDAY		
THURSDAY		
FRIDAY		
SATURDAY		

WEEK 1: Reflecting on Life's Lessons.

Personal: _______________________________________

____

____

____

Professional: _______________________________________

____

____

____

Spiritual: _______________________________________

____

____

____

WEEK 2: Embracing Growth and Change.

Personal: _______________________________

____

____

____

____

Professional: _______________________________

____

____

____

____

Spiritual: _______________________________

____

____

____

WEEK 3: Acknowledging Strengths and Vulnerabilities.

Personal: ____

____

____

____

____

Professional: ____

____

____

____

____

Spiritual: ____

____

____

____

WEEK 4: Celebrating Achievements and Preparing for New Beginnings.

Personal: ____

____

____

____

____

Professional: ____

____

____

____

Spiritual: ____

____

____

____

WEEK 5: Setting Intentions for the Coming Year.
(For 5-week months)

Personal: ____

____

____

____

Professional: ____

____

____

____

Spiritual: ____

____

____

____

PERSONAL GOALS

Track three personal goals related to the theme of fulfillment for the month. Encourage reflection on how these goals capture the year's learning and growth, and how they will guide the journey into the new year.

Goal 1: ____

____

____

____

Goal 2: ____

____

____

____

Goal 3: ____

____

____

____

CALENDAR

MONTH/YEAR: _________________

Sunday	Monday	Tuesday	Wednesday	Thursday	Friday	Saturday

- NOTES -

- NOTES -

- NOTES -

- NOTES -

- NOTES -

- NOTES -

- NOTES -

I can do all things through Christ
that strengthen me.
Phil. 4:13 KJV